AN
AFTER-SCHOOL
WORKBOOK
FOR FIRST AND SECOND
GRADERS WITH AUTISM

An
AFTER-SCHOOL
WORKBOOK
for FIRST and SECOND
GRADERS with AUTISM

BY DAWN ADAMS

AN AFTER-SCHOOL WORKBOOK FOR FIRST AND SECOND GRADERS WITH AUTISM

iUniverse books may be ordered through booksellers or by contacting:

iUniverse
1663 Liberty Drive
Bloomington, IN 47403
www.iuniverse.com
1-800-Authors (1-800-288-4677)

Because of the dynamic nature of the Internet, any web addresses or links contained in this book may have changed since publication and may no longer be valid. The views expressed in this work are solely those of the author and do not necessarily reflect the views of the publisher, and the publisher hereby disclaims any responsibility for them.

Any people depicted in stock imagery provided by Thinkstock are models, and such images are being used for illustrative purposes only. Certain stock imagery © Thinkstock.

ISBN: 978-1-4917-7091-7 (sc)
ISBN: 978-1-4917-7090-0 (e)

Print information available on the last page.

iUniverse rev. date: 12/2/2015

CONTENTS

SPELLING

HISTORY

SPORTS

ANIMALS

HOLIDAYS

VEHICLES

PEOPLE

SHORT STORIES

OUR SON, BILLY

When our son, Billy, was diagnosed with autism, we knew little of this widespread condition, which is becoming more common. Since then, through conducting intensive research, going to meetings, and speaking with hundreds of others, we've realized the devastation and heartbreak of this horrific condition.

I took Billy to school on his very first day. He was soon to be four years old. Billy was hesitant at first, but as he was getting into the classroom, he was really enjoying being around the other children. During the first few months of school, I would hide in his classroom from time to time to see how he was really doing.

Every morning, I would start my routine with Billy. I'd wake him up, get him dressed for school, cook his breakfast, brush his hair and his teeth, wash his hands and face, and put on his backpack. Billy would always stand in front of the picture window and wait for the school bus to come up the street. He'd be so excited when the bus came to the house. He would throw his arms up and down in excitement and have the biggest smile on his face. And then I would walk him to the school bus, kiss him, and wait for the bus to leave. Mostly out of sight.

And when Billy came home from school, I would always have a snack ready for him. While he was eating, I would read everything the teachers had sent home in his book bag. For the first few years, the teachers would send each child home with a progress report on how he or she did that day, including what he or she responded to and didn't respond to. I would spend more time with him in that particular area. In each class, there would be one teacher and at least one teacher's aide. I would continue with whatever else they'd been teaching that day.

However, we started to notice that the following day reports were on subjects totally different from the day before. They were teaching these classes as though they were regular classrooms instead of special-needs classes.

Most special-needs children cannot comprehend anything as fast as children in regular classrooms. I realized that they had to move on, but the next day seemed too soon. From talking with several parents from different areas, I discovered that a lot of teachers aren't really qualified to teach children with special needs. I don't think they're bad teachers; they are just not special-needs teachers. Some teachers do not have the patience needed to teach them.

A lot of special-needs children need one-on-one attention. That's why a teacher's aide is in the classroom. Also, special-needs children have very limited attention spans. Getting children to stay interested for ten to fifteen minutes at a time is great when you are teaching them. You have to have a lot of patience, which is very important. A lot of the time, you will have to go over the same thing over and over again until they grasp the concept. I realize teachers don't have the time to do this all day on a daily basis, but from what I have witnessed, the teacher's aides could help out in that area—and a lot more. I am not talking about *all* aides.

I've also witnessed that special-needs children are also different when it comes to their learning abilities. There may be a class with just special-needs children, all around the same age, and some of them will learn faster or slower than the others.

Every year, Billy gets tested to determine his mental age. Unfortunately, Billy has always been a few years behind. We learned that he doesn't mentally grow a year every year. In his case, we were told he only grows about six or seven months mentally.

When Billy was in fifth grade, we noticed the special-needs children were being taught as if they were eight to ten years old when mentally they were four to six years old and still learning subjects being taught in first grade.

Every parent or grandparent I have spoken with over the years tells me the same thing when their children or grandchildren start school. When they meet the teachers for the first time, they tell them in detail about the medical problems their children or grandchildren have that the teachers need to be aware of. The teachers write the medical problems in their files. From time to time, the parents or grandparents send notes or letters or even make phone calls to the teachers to remind them about their children's needs when they notice something hasn't been done.

Unfortunately in Billy's case, he was progressing slowly. Even though the school system kept moving him up every year, we still had to go over everything until he caught on and understood.

The school systems in our country are getting worse instead of better. State agencies aren't funding for special-needs children like they once were. Billy hasn't come home with any reports for a few years. Unless we called the teachers or sat in his classroom, we wouldn't know what was being taught right then. I started writing these workbooks so parents can get all the information in one book instead of having to shop at different places for different materials. I published *The Needs of Billy and Other Autistic Children* for parents of kindergarteners. The parents can use the same material for however long it takes to teach their children before having to move on.

Children also love stuffed animals. For children who cannot talk, buy stuffed animals that will help them imitate the sound of words.

One way to improve their skills is to play with toys that draw their attention to who is speaking. You want to get—and keep—their attention. If you pass the animal back and forth, they will know who is in control right then.

We have found it very important to praise special-needs children a lot after they learn something for the first time. We would tell Billy over and over how proud we were of him. Then we would clap and say, "Great going, Billy." We would do it for at least thirty seconds, and Billy would always show how happy he was. He would giggle, swing his arms up and down, and do his little dance. We would always kiss on him for about a minute. Billy rarely pulled away when I'd kiss on him. I was so happy he didn't mind when I would do that.

When he was learning how to write, we would hold our hands over and draw the same letter over and over and over until he could do it by himself. This required a lot of patience. When you start teaching special-needs children sign language, don't be upset if it takes months or years. Always keep in mind that their attention spans are very limited. But when they learn, they usually remember it for good.

When Billy doesn't want to do anything he already knows how to do, he'll pretend not to know how to do it. That's when you have to be stern. Of course, I would let him get away with it, but not very often. I always have to remind myself it's really for his own good.

At Christmastime, when all the presents were under the tree, Billy never went near them. He was only excited about the tree, the lights, and the ornaments. When it was time to open the presents, he never reacted with excitement. He only reacted with excitement when he saw a toy or a stuffed animal. The more sounds it made or the more colors he saw, the more excitement he showed. Just like with other children. When he saw clothes or books, he had no reaction, but when he saw a toy, he was very excited.

SPECIAL-NEEDS CHILDREN

When I started looking for support for Billy at home, I found it very difficult. After years of research, I have learned a lot from watching him in classrooms, outside, and at home. I am not a teacher. I'm a mother who is looking for answers. After watching Billy over the years, I pretty much learned everything about his wants and needs. I hope this will help you out as much as it helped me.

Being individuals, we all require special help at some point in our lives. Special-needs children will soon grow up and develop into adults. They need to learn what appropriate behavior is—and what it is not—to help them move forward.

Imagine what it would be like if you were somewhere new and were unable to speak or understand directions. This is what it is like for most special-needs children. It can be very frightening.

THINGS TO REMEMBER

Your child may exhibit

- lack of communicating skills;
- lack of imaginative and creative play; or
- difficulty making friends.

Your child may be

- polite;
- caring;
- knowledgeable about a particular subject; or
- great at math, music, or arts.

SELF-REFLECTION

- How am I speaking to my child?
- Never use sarcasm, because autistic children are very literal.

- Does the autistic child understand my instructions?
- Am I being clear and precise?

SOCIALIZING

It is not automatic for autistic children to know how to talk to others; they need to be told, sometimes repeatedly. They may, when meeting people, kiss them in greeting or want to touch them. They need to know what is appropriate. Other students may find some of the autistic pupil's behavior disturbing. These children need to be aware that the autistic classmate is not being deliberately rude or unkind; an autistic child may have difficulty understanding the right way to behave. You need to tell your child that inappropriate behavior is upsetting the other students. Hopefully his or her peer group will help him or her in this situation if they understand.

It is a great idea to make a chart at home and in the classroom with some opening lines:

- Do you have a hobby?
- What did you do over the weekend?
- Have the teacher appoint a buddy to help.

STRUCTURE

Special-needs students like structure. They like to know what is going to happen and when. Change can upset them greatly. Autistic children find it really hard to make choices.

MAKING IT EASIER

- When teaching your child at home, write down the tasks, and tape them next to where you will be teaching the child.
- Give him/her a written timetable.
- If you are about to change something, let him or her know ahead of time.
- In class, have a buddy help the child.

PLAYTIME

Autistic children don't understand there are rules on the playground. They find it hard to play with other children. They like to play by themselves or walk around and make loud noises. Without planning ahead, difficulties may arise with other children.

FREE MIND AT PLAYTIME

- Take your child to a park where there are other children. Talk to your child about how to behave toward other children.
- Let your child take some special toys to the park.
- Show your child how to share.

OBSESSIONS

- Some children display obsessional behavior, such as collecting paper clips, little tops, or buttons.
- Some children love to walk up and down in the room. In class, this may become disruptive.

USING THE OBSESSION

If your child likes moving about in the classroom, give the child a task to do. Perhaps give the teacher a note. Let the teacher know ahead of time that this may happen from time to time.

TALK TO THE TEACHER

Talk to your child's teacher about inappropriate behavior and physical or verbal mistakes that might occur. Remind the teacher to praise the child whenever appropriate behavior happens.

- It is never good to say, "Don't do that" or "Stop it."
- If you have asked the child not to do something, explain what you want the child to do.

- If something goes wrong, give calm, clear alternatives.
- Be open about any social slipups.

ONE TO ONE

Working individually with a student is great, but be careful that your child doesn't become dependent on one adult. It is important that your child works and plays with his or her own peer group to enable full integration during school years. This will allow him or her to move into adulthood with the necessary skills for everyday life.

WORDS FROM AUTISTIC CHILDREN

In my other book, I talked about going to other schools to learn about teaching my son at home after school. I was fortunate enough to learn what other autistic children wanted as well. Very few autistic children can talk, but the ones who can are able to communicate a few things they desire—or would like others to know:

- I want friends.
- I want people to like me.
- I am good at a lot of things.

I HEAR THINGS MORE LOUDLY.

I SEE THINGS MORE CLEARLY.

I SMELL THINGS MORE STRONGLY.

I FEEL THINGS YOU DON'T.

I TASTE THINGS DIFFERENTLY.

I HAVE AUTISM.

UNDERSTANDING AUTISM

Autism is an increasingly more common neurological condition that affects brain development. Children diagnosed with autism tend to have more difficulty socializing, communicating effectively, and responding appropriately to their environments.

Every child is unique. How autism affects one child is often very different from how it affects another. Children with autism possess a wide variety of skills, strengths, interests, and needs. An individualized approach to education, training, and support can play an important role in the development of a child with autism.

There are simple ways to support the development. In addition to educational strategies and targeted therapy, there are simple, everyday steps that parents, teachers, and caregivers can take to support children with autism.

- Talk to children in advance about the day's scheduled activities to help children know what to expect.
- Create a schedule that includes picture symbols for daily activities, and check them off as they're completed.
- Give children choices, such as which clothes to wear or which drawing tools to use, to give them a sense of control.
- Encourage children to use appropriate ways to communicate their needs rather than using behavioral responses.
- Build on children's strengths, and use their special interests to motivate learning.

LEARNING FROM BILLY

From the day Billy was born, I've been learning from him as well. Billy has taught me that children are children. Special-needs children have the same basic needs as other children. They are curious. They love to play with toys, go to zoos, and play in parks. They love to watch cartoons and look at books with a lot of colorful pictures. They want to learn.

Special-needs children should be given activities they like and activities they can do. They need to experience success and failure. Special-needs children may require special care based on their unique needs, but I believe it's very important they are not treated any differently.

Through the years of being around a lot of special-needs children and young adults, I've learned that, in most cases, these children can do more than they can't do.

With Billy, we tried planning out activities ahead of time. We would teach him in simple steps and praise and encourage him as he learned. I had to remind myself to use his name instead of calling him *sweetie, baby cakes*, and so forth. I made sure he was always paying attention to us. We would use directions. Before starting an activity, we would show and tell him how the activity would be done. We would tell him the name of everything we would be using. When needed, we would put our hands over his to guide him through each step.

We never rushed Billy to complete anything. We never forced him to do tasks beyond his ability.

All children learn by doing. Billy does well with other children, which is great because they learn from each other. The field trips he went on were valuable.

I would watch Billy in class, and I would attend other classes in other schools. I noticed that special-needs children with other medical problems would be restricted from most of the learning activities. These other needs should not prevent them from participating in activities that would help them learn. When doctor prescribe medicine or bed rest, teachers should go over the activities with the parents so the children will not fall behind.

At one of the schools I visited, the teacher was wonderful. She was teaching first grade. At lunchtime, the class was having lunch in the classroom instead of the cafeteria. She had all eight students get in line, walk to the kitchen area to get plates and utensils, walk back to the table, lay everything down on the table where they should be sitting, get back in line, get their cups for milk, walk back to the table, sit down, and wait for the teacher's aide to bring them their lunches. After they finished eating, they got back in line, put their plates and cups in the trash bin, and put the utensils in the sink. They walked back to the table, sat down, and waited for the teacher to tell them what to do next.

After a few weeks, I had him setting the table. He enjoyed doing it. Every night, we would clap our hands and tell him what a great job he was doing. We would set the table the same way every night so he knew where everything would be. Soon after that, we started giving him some chores. However, making his bed was not on his fun list. It took almost a month, but he started doing it.

Since Billy started his chores, he falls asleep much faster. I think it's because he's afraid we will ask him to do more chores!

Billy was never one to exercise. He never has cared for it. After dinner, his daddy would usually take him outside to walk around the block. It took months before he would walk around the entire block without being held part of the way. Billy's doctor suggested exercises to strengthen his muscles. During the summer, he's always in the pool. He loves playing and swimming in the pool. Billy learned how to swim when he was six years old.

Billy seems happier when he's around several people, especially other children. We put him in groups to build his social skills. He likes to read, play with a few other children, play in his pool, and listen to music. Billy loves music.

He has a three-foot frog that dances. He's had it for years. When we bought it a year ago, we noticed how much he loved it. We ordered another one for backup.

TECHNIQUES WE USE WITH BILLY

Encourage communication. We use visual aids as much as possible: pictures, sign language, and gestures.

Comprehension. We avoid talking as if he isn't present. We involve Billy in conversations even when we don't get responses. We give him a lot of time to respond.

Structure and routine. We make small changes to his routine to see how much he can tolerate.

Guiding versus pushing. Many children with autism are very resistant to change, and they may to be fixated on certain subjects or objects. These qualities can be used to motivate children to improve attention, communication, and social skills.

TEACHING AT HOME

It was much easier for me to learn sign language before teaching someone else. I was constantly looking back and forth. Also, in our experience, autistic children easily forget if you're not going over and over the same thing before they fully understand what you are teaching.

Special-needs children have very short attention spans. I have witnessed children being taught on a one-on-one basis. The teachers or aides would teach for fifteen minutes and then let the child rest for about five minutes. The charts and illustrations in this book were being taught in all the schools I have visited.

All children try to distract you and keep you from continuing. Billy knew exactly how to get me to stop teaching and just play. He would just smile from ear to ear or start laughing for no reason. It worked for a few minutes, but then I had to show him it was not time to play.

We gave him a snack when he got home from school. Giving him a small snack and then playing with him for about ten or fifteen minutes before we sat him down to begin teaching was very beneficial.

MOTIVATING BILLY TO WRITE

Billy loves to color with crayons, but he does not like to write. Keeping a pencil in his hand was always a challenge. To help motivate Billy, I would start out with a pencil. After a few minutes, I would let him change from the pencil to one of the following:

- a magic marker
- pen or pencil with a creature wiggling over the eraser
- colored pens or pencils
- finger paint (when doing numbers)
- pens with glittery ink
- markers that smell sweet
- watercolors
- finger crayons (we put the crayon over his fingers)
- chalk (writing on the chalkboard)

The small chalkboard was his favorite.

CHOOSING THE BEST TOYS

When we bought Billy toys for learning, we considered his developmental needs. To keep him interested as long as possible, we made playtime fun and educational.

Playing board games with your children will keep their interest. Take them outside as often as you can to play ball. Have your child catch the ball as often as possible.

Most children love dress up—the younger, the better. Halloween is a great time to begin because they get excited about dressing up and going trick or treating.

Also try pretending with your children. Little boys like playing pretend just as much as little girls do. Little girls like pretending to be mommies; make sure you have little dolls, dollhouses, doll clothing, strollers, and so forth, for your little girl. If your child wants to pretend to be a baker, buy an Easy-Bake Oven, little pots and pans, and plastic condiments so they can play the role. (If you use an Easy-Bake Oven, make sure you or someone else in the house can be there with them because they are electric and get very warm.)

If your child wants to be a police officer or a firefighter, get the outfits and amenities they need to carry out their roles.

SENSORY INPUT

For the past thirteen years, I have read hundreds of reports on sensory processing disorder with autism. I would read everything I could get my hands on to help my son. Even though the latest information has not changed, I am still waiting for a miracle.

However, according to ***Psychology Today***, I haven't learned of any new ways to help my son. Most people who suffer from autism also suffer from sensory processing disorder.

This affects an individual's ability to filter out extraneous sensory information, such as a dog barking or another child talking. This also leads children to performing stereotypical repetitive behavior portion of the autism diagnostic criteria.

This over and under activity can make it difficult for a child with autism to focus on any task, including learning to read.

Over the years I've learned that the following ideas can help a child regulate his or her sensory system and focus on reading.

- Try reading in a quiet, sensory neutral space, such as a dimly lit room with no artwork on the walls. Either sit close together—or sit on the floor—and speak in a slow, quiet voice.
- Try identifying whether the child is dealing with too much stimulation or not enough stimulation—or maybe both. Some occupational therapists suggest tools, such as vibrating pencil grips, chew toys, or other products to help children focus on learning.
- Many children learn better when they are moving. Sometimes we put our son in a swing or a rocking chair. He loves both.

IMPROVING ORAL MOTOR SKILLS

- tape recorder
- bubbles
- musical wind instruments
- whistles

FOR IMPROVING HAND STRENGTH

- dough
- clay
- art toys for fine motor skills
- colored pencils
- colored/plain paper
- crayons
- markers
- paintbrushes
- paint

INDOOR TOYS FOR MONITORING SKILLS

- large balls (for hopping)
- tents
- tunnels

Taking frequent breaks will provide the sensory stimulation the child craves. Try reading for ten minutes before a five minute break or working for fifteen minutes before a ten minute break. Although the break times may seem too frequent or too long, the child **will** make progress.

PAGE FOR PARENTS

The activities in this book are for first and second grade students. There are words to read, easy activities to do, new things to learn, and math problems to solve. With this book it will help your child keep up with the pace of other children.

- Pick a comfortable spot to work in - one with plenty of light.
- Choose a time when your child is able to concentrate.
- Gather crayons, pencils or markers and get your child ready to fill in the spaces on the pages.
- Read the words aloud to your child. Listen to them. Point to the pictures. Laugh at them. Words and pictures are fun, and fun is good.
- Words and numbers are here, there and everywhere! When you're driving in your car with your child along a familiar route, read the signs aloud.
- And remember, children develop at different paces. These activities were created for first and second grade children with AUTISM, but this is only a guide.

PAGE FOR PARENTS

Add on to the list what else works for your child and children.

1

2

3

4

5

6

7

8

9

10

SENSORY AND MOTOR SKILLS

SNACKS

- What does it taste like?
- Is it sweet?
- Is it sour?
- Is it bitter?
- Is it salty?

SPREADABLES

Have your child spread peanut butter, jelly, or cheese on crackers or bread.
   At home, we have Billy do these activities:

- popping bubble wrap
- crumbling paper
- squeezing over and over play dough
- cutting using scissors
- blowing bubbles (his favorite)
- jumping up and down on a two-foot trampoline

SENSORY TOYS FOR INTEGRATION

- sand table
- hanging rings
- musical instruments
- drums
- rattles
- small toys

BUILDING TOYS (INDOORS OR OUTSIDE)

- Legos
- Tinkertoys
- blocks (for the big blocks, they now make them out of cardboard)

TRIGGERS OF BEHAVIOR

- noise
- strangers
- pace
- proximity
- change of routine
- capacity
- demands
- stressful
- chaos
- being ignored

WHEN CHILDREN ARE NOT PAYING ATTENTION

- Ask them to repeat what you said.
- Stand next to them.
- Get up and move around.
- Find out what excites them, and add something related.

VOLUME METER

What places are you to be quiet?
What places can you whisper?
What places can you talk?
What places can you talk with raised voices?
What places can you talk very loud?

church	parties
recess	class
movies	library
cheering	ball games
restaurant	talking

KEEP A JOURNAL

We always watched Billy and took notes, noting what he focused on (his favorite things).

We noticed what he was doing when he was the happiest and where he could excel.

We read books about autism. We would set goals for him and start working backward. It didn't matter if it looked different than traditional schooling. We would always set goals, work toward those goals, and document his progress.

At times, we would change course by letting him show us how he learned best. We also had home therapy for him.

YOUR BODY

Name each part of your body on the lines below. Where are your ears, hands, elbows, wrists, hands, chest, knees, ankles, shoulders, and toes?

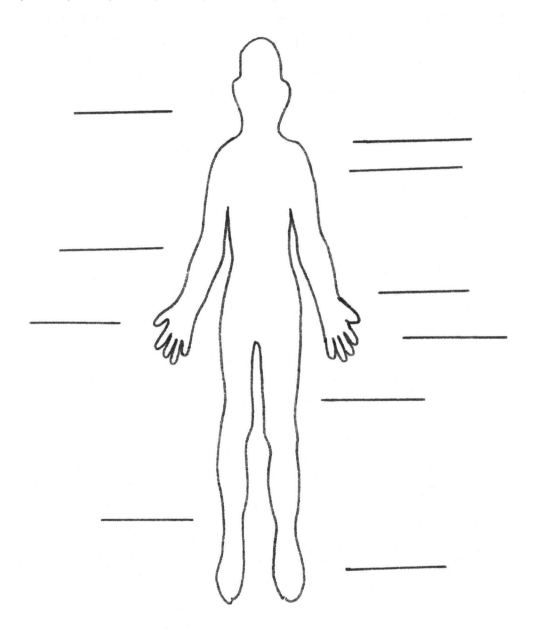

DRESSING YOURSELF

What would you put on *first*, a shirt or a coat? What would you put on *second*, a shirt or a coat?

DRESSING YOURSELF

What would you put on *first*, your underwear or your pants? What would you put on *second*, your underwear or your pants?

DRESSING YOURSELF

What do you put on your feet *first*? Then what do you put on *next*?

MY MEASUREMENTS

Have an adult use a measuring tape to help you measure these parts of your body.

My hand is about _____ inches long.

My foot is about _____ inches wide.

My arm from shoulder to wrist is _____ inches long.

My shoulders are _____ inches wide.

My leg from hip to knee is _____ inches long.

My leg from knee to ankle is _____ inches long.

My head is _____ inches around.

My face is _____ inches long and _____ inches wide.

I _____, am inches tall.

HANDS

Is this your right or your left hand?

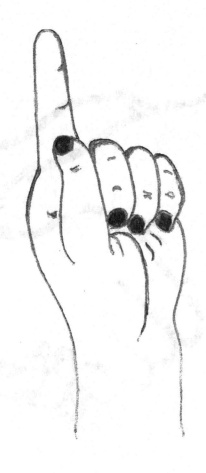

HANDS

Are they shaking hands or holding hands?

WASH HANDS

turn tap on	get soap
scrub hands	rinse hands
turn tap off	dry hands

STEP-BY-STEP POTTY TRAINING

Hang over the toilet so your child can see it and read it every day.

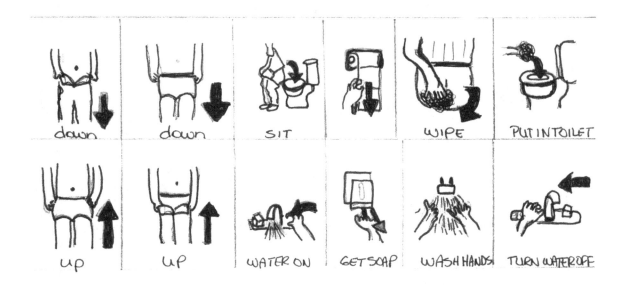

down	down	SIT		WIPE	PUT IN TOILET
UP	UP	WATER ON	GET SOAP	WASH HANDS	TURN WATER OFF

Put an *X* next to the ones you don't do when swimming.

- Put your head under before holding your breath.
- On your first day, dive off the diving board.
- On the side of the pool, practice kicking your feet.
- Jump in the pool when you are laughing.
- Have someone hold his or her arms out so you can practice kicking your feet and paddling your arms.
- On the first day you are learning how to swim, jump in the deep end.
- When learning how to swim, never go swimming alone.
- Have someone who doesn't know how to swim as your swimming instructor.
- Hold your breath when going underwater.

American Sign Language
Finger Spelling Chart

A	B	C	D
E	F	G	H
I	J	K	L
M	N	O	P
Q	R	S	T
U	V	W	X
Y	Z		

WHAT ARE THE LETTERS BELOW?

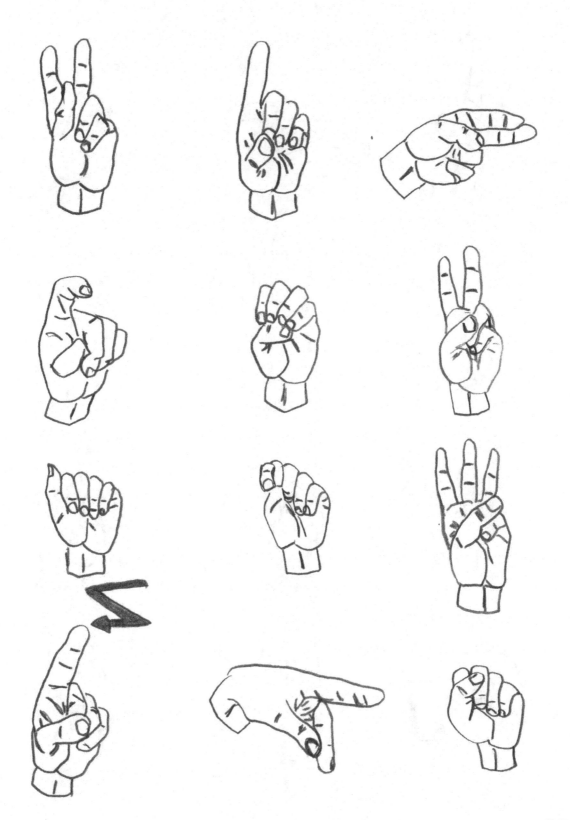

WHAT ARE THE LETTERS BELOW?

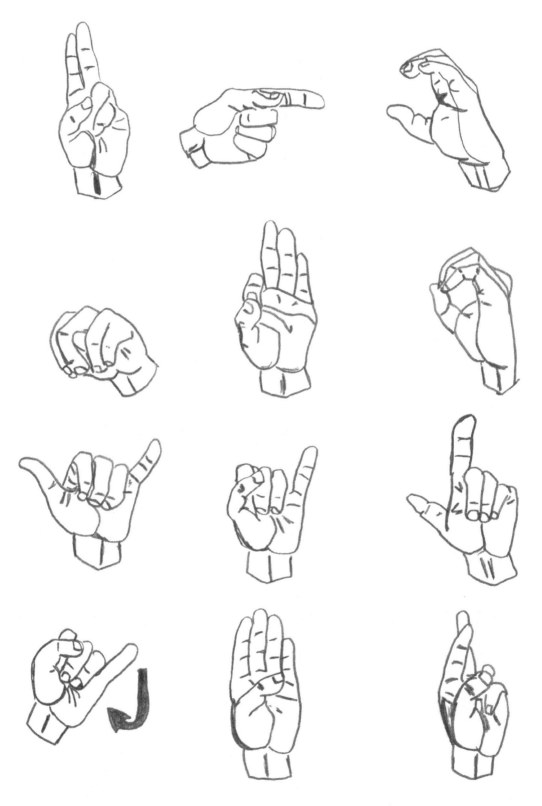

WHAT ARE THE LETTERS BELOW?

CAN YOU SAY THESE LETTERS?

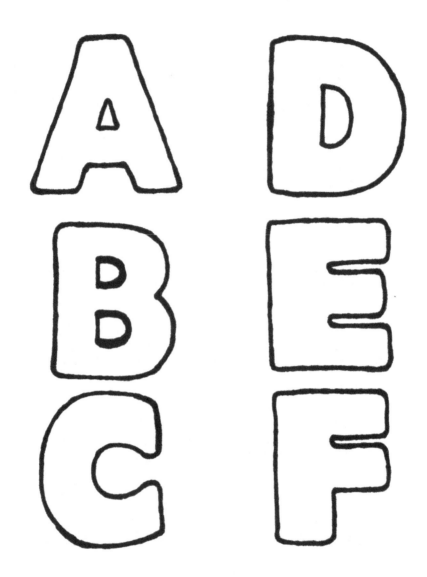

CAN YOU SAY THESE LETTERS?

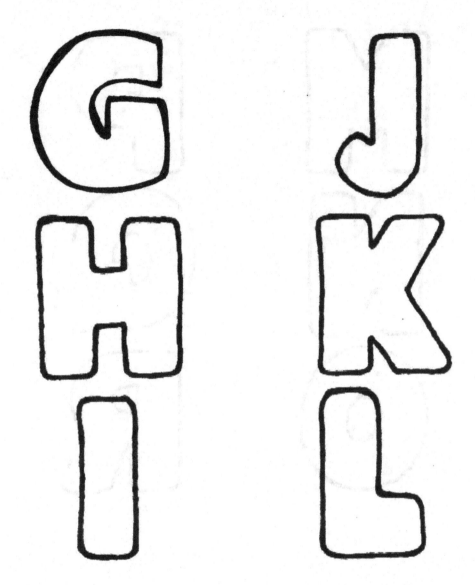

CAN YOU SAY THESE LETTERS?

CAN YOU SAY THESE LETTERS?

CAN YOU SAY THESE LETTERS?

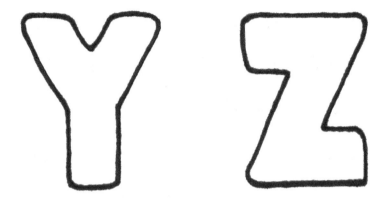

LETTERS

What is the first letter that each picture begins with?

LETTERS

What is the first letter that each picture begins with?

LETTERS

What is the first letter that each picture begins with?

___   ___

___

___   ___

___

SIGHT WORDS

ask	every
when	high
live	right
day	house
would	thank
some	could
then	again

SIGHT WORDS

how	also
many	where
back	their
about	learn
after	work
here	long
been	each

SIGHT WORDS

Choose a word from below. Use a word to complete each sentence.

after   made   soon   that   from   help
your   give   brown   under   know   find

Did you _____ my red hat.

My shoes are _____ the bed.

The dog has _____ fur.

I like to _____ cook dinner.

Is that _____ favorite book?

I made _____ a tasty snack.

MEMORY-MATCHING GAME

Help expand your child's memory. Challenge your child with a fun memory-matching game with sight words.

thank	high
again	when
high	thank
when	again

MEMORY-MATCHING GAME

Help expand your child's memory. Challenge your child with a fun memory-matching game with sight words.

could	house
would	where
house	could
where	would

MEMORY-MATCHING GAME

Help expand your child's memory. Challenge your child with a fun memory-matching game with sight words.

some	right
how	some
live	how
right	live

MEMORY-MATCHING GAME

Help expand your child's memory. Challenge your child with a fun memory-matching game with sight words.

each	back
then	learn
back	each
learn	then

MEMORY-MATCHING GAME

Help expand your child's memory. Challenge your child with a fun memory-matching game with sight words.

here	day
been	work
work	here
day	been

SUMMER READING

As the school year ends, be sure to congratulate your child on a job well done! During the summer, encourage your child to continue reading. Reading is a perfect way to relax, and it is a great way to ensure your child is prepared for the next grade level.

On the following page, there is a list of books and movies to capture and keep your child's attention. For children who are not ready to read yet, take a few minutes each night to read aloud to them.

To reinforce comprehension, pause occasionally to ask about various characters or events in the story, Ask one or two questions to help the child make connections in what you have just read.

- What was your favourite part?
- Who was your favourite character and why?
- Did you like the way that it ended?
- How would you change the story?

BOOKS

- The cat in the Hat
- The complete tales and poems of: Winnie the Pooh
- Charlie and the Chocolate Factory
- Charlotte's Web
- Harry Potter and the Sorcerer's Stone
- Alice's Adventures in Wonderland
- Diary of a Wimpy Kid
- I am Malala
- Wonder

MOVIES

- Curious George – The Boo fest
- Toy Story
- Beauty and the Beast
- Finding Nemo
- My Neighbor Totoro
- Babe
- Mary Poppins
- Shrek
- E.T.
- Star Wars – Episode IV: A New Hope

Where do students return their books
when they are finished with them?

KNOWING THE WEATHER
RAIN SUN SNOW HAIL TORNADO

What is happening when you see or feel water drops from the sky?

What is shining so bright when the skies are clear and blue?

What are white small flakes falling from the ski?

What is a very dark cloud that goes round and round and produces a lot of strong winds?

What are the small white balls of ice coming from the ski?

YOUR ANSWERS BELOW

1. _____
2. _____
3. _____
4. _____
5. _____

SUN

The sun is a very hot star.
It gives the earth heat, light, and energy.

MOONS

WIND

Wind is the air moving in different directions.

SINK OR FLOAT

Which items will sink, and which items will float?

CEMENT BLOCK

SINK OR FLOAT

Which items will sink, and which items will float?

Which items below will sink or float?

BUG IDENTIFICATION

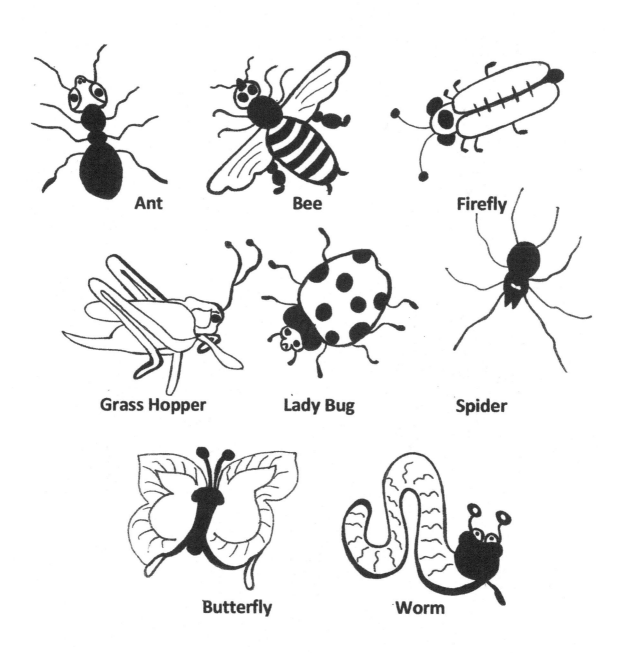

Ant

Bee

Firefly

Grass Hopper

Lady Bug

Spider

Butterfly

Worm

LIFE CYCLE OF A PLANT

How do plants grow?
Can you put the pots in the correct order?

SPROUT

WATER

SOIL

SUNLIGHT

PLANT

SEEDS

MATH

Find the circles in each picture.
Write down how many you find on the line.
How many circles are there? _____

MATH

Find the eyes in each picture.
Write down how many you find on the line.
How many eyes are there? _____

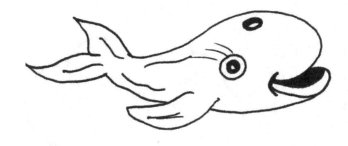

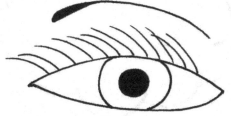

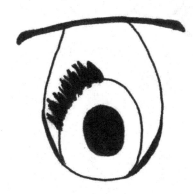

MATH

Find the circles in each picture.
Write down how many you find on the line underneath.
How many circles are there? _____

NUMBER SORTING

How many flowerpots have the number 7 on them?

How many flowerpots have the number 1 on them?

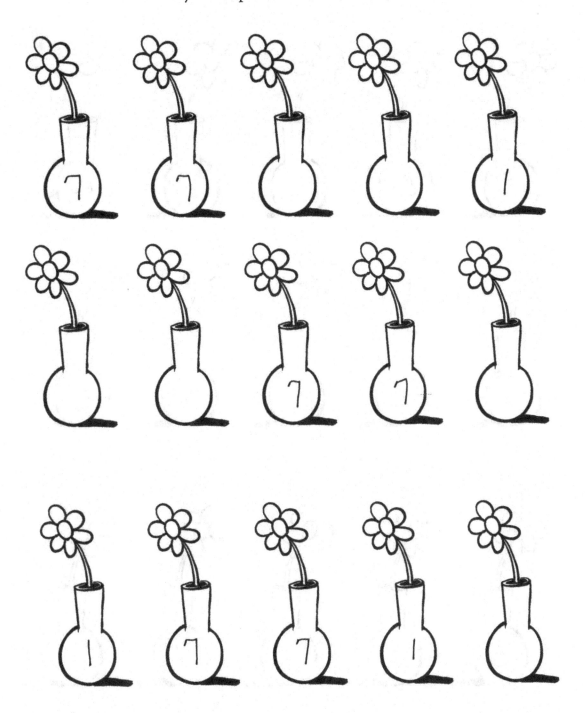

NUMBER SORTING

How many flowerpots have the number 4 on them?
How many flowerpots have the number 5 on them?

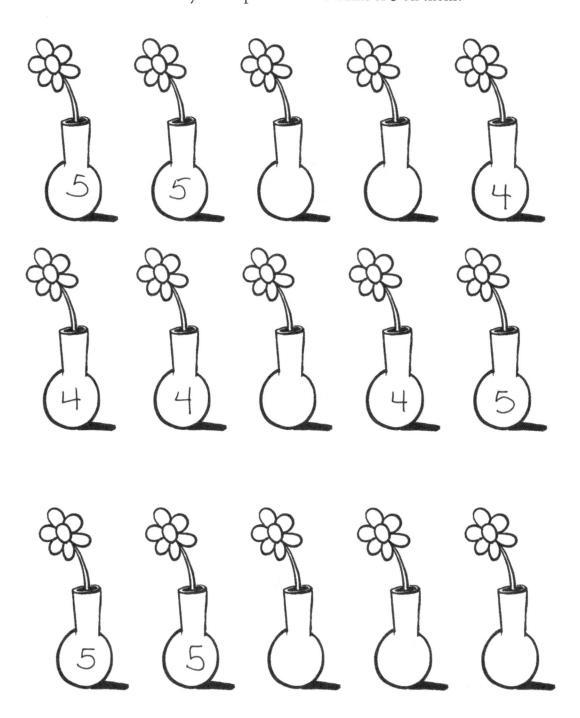

NUMBER SORTING

How many flowerpots have the number 2 on them?
How many flowerpots have the number 8 on them?

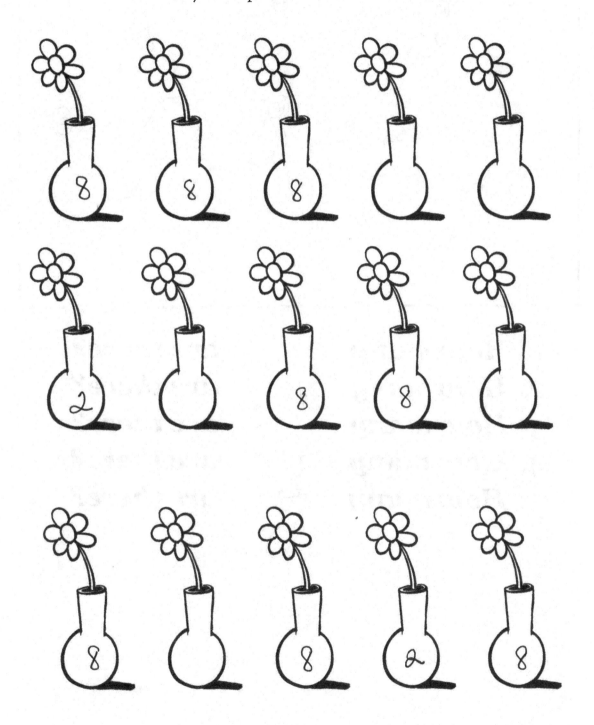

COUNTING FUN

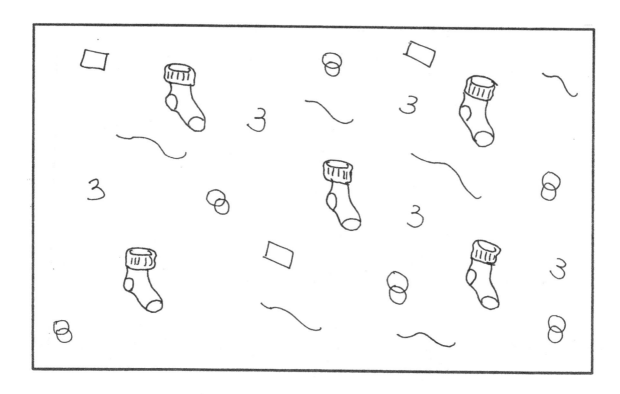

1. How many 3 are there?
2. How many ▭ are there?
3. How many  are there?
4. How many ◯◯ are there?
5. How many [sock image] are there?

COUNTING FUN

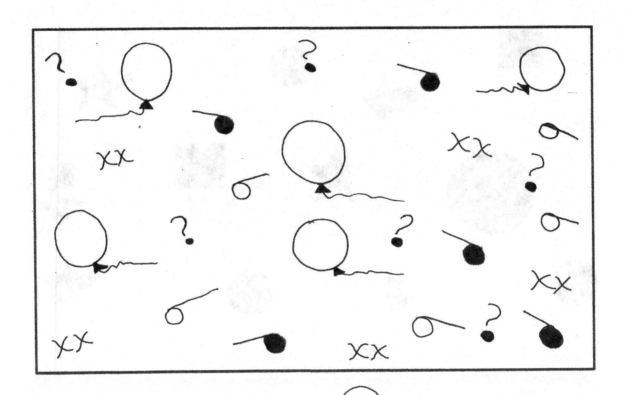

1. How many ![balloon] are there?
2. How many ![o] are there?
3. How many ![dot] are there?
4. How many xx are there?
5. How many ? are there?

COUNTING FUN

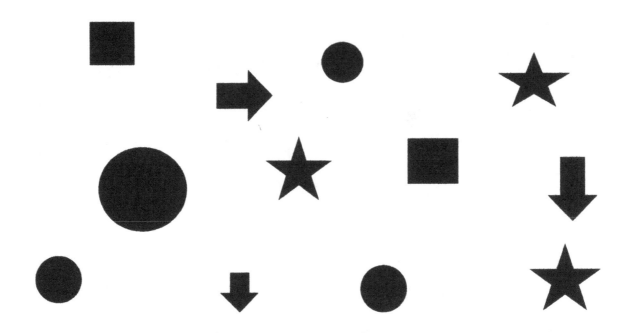

How many ⬤ are there?

How many ⬇ are there?

How many ★ are there?

How many ■ are there?

SHARP JUMBLE

Which ones are circles?
Which ones are triangles?
Which ones are squares?

THE NUMBER ONE

Count the buttons on each shirt.
How many shirts have one button?

THE NUMBER ONE

Count the buttons on each shirt.
How many shirts have one button?

COMPARING-QUANTITES QUIZ

Which two squares have _less_ than the amount in the first square?

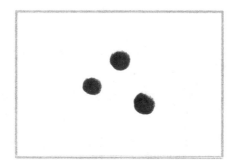

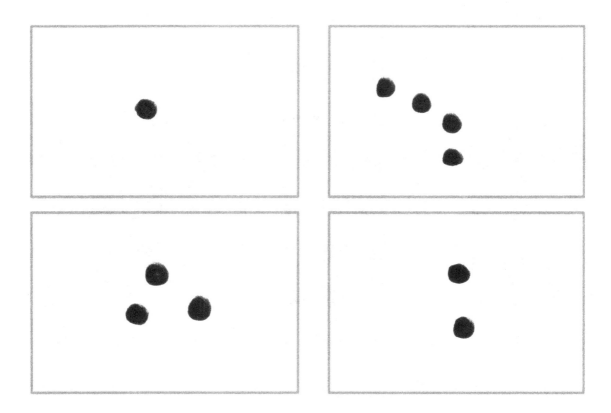

COMPARING-QUANTITES QUIZ

Which two squares have _less_ than the amount in the first square?

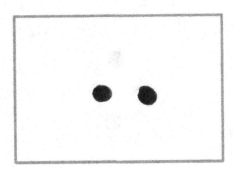

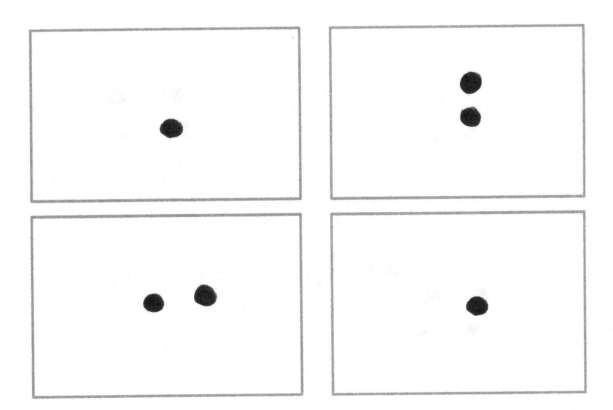

COMPARING-QUANTITES QUIZ

Which two squares have _less_ than the amount in the first square?

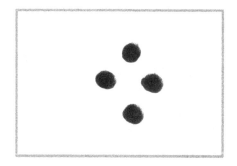

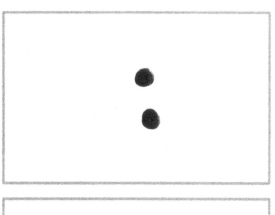

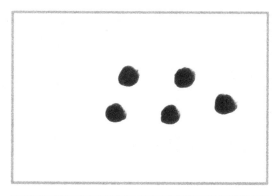

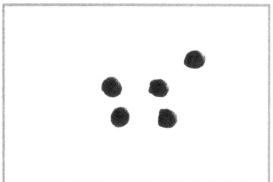

COMPARING-QUANTITES QUIZ

Which two squares have _more_ than the amount in the first square?

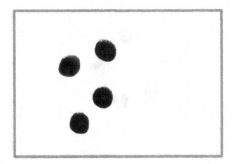

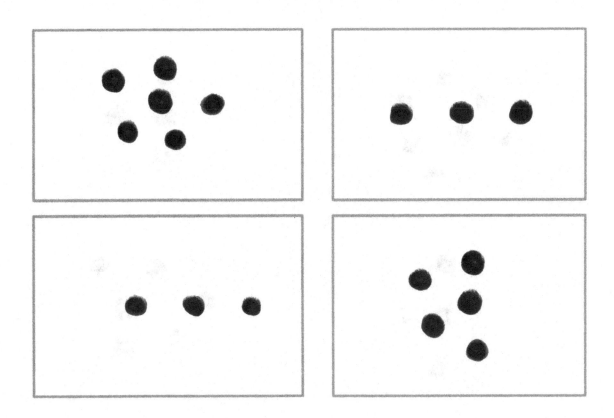

COMPARING-QUANTITES QUIZ

Which two squares have _more_ than the amount in the first square?

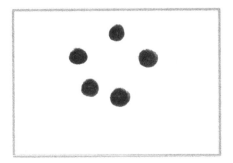

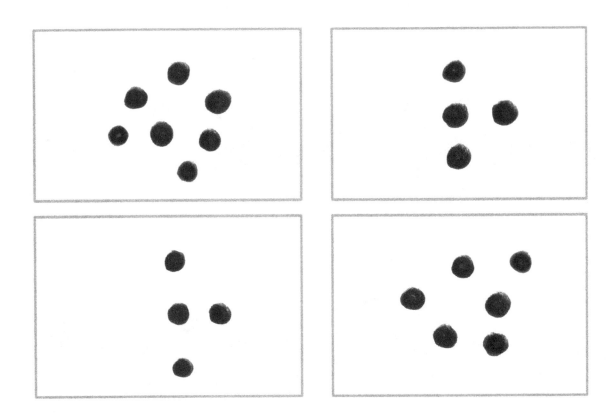

COMPARING-QUANTITES QUIZ

Which two squares have _more_ than the amount in the first square?

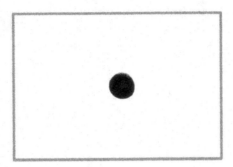

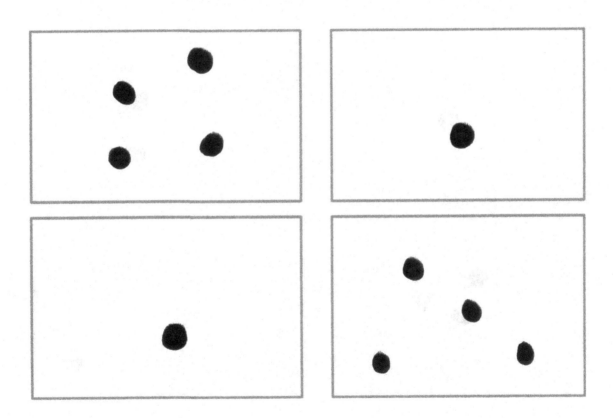

COMPARING-QUANTITES QUIZ

Which two squares have the _same_ amount as the first square?

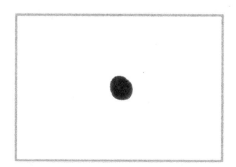

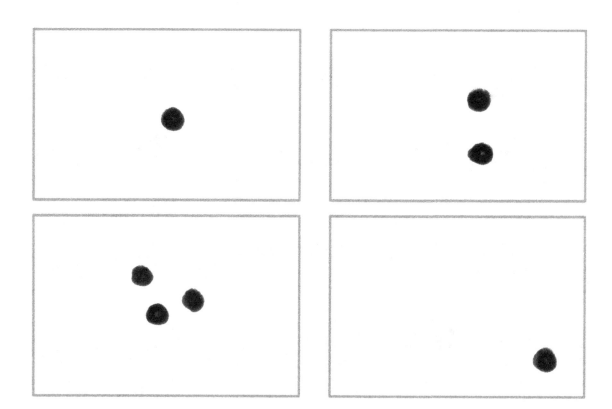

COMPARING-QUANTITES QUIZ

Which two squares have the _same_ amount as the first square?

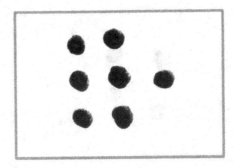

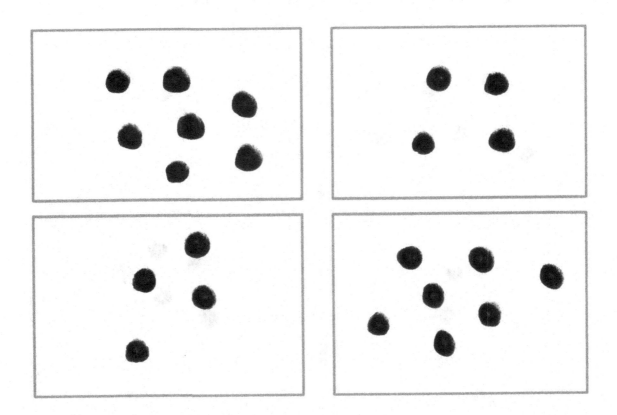

COMPARING-QUANTITES QUIZ

Which two squares have the _same_ amount as the first square?

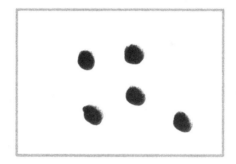

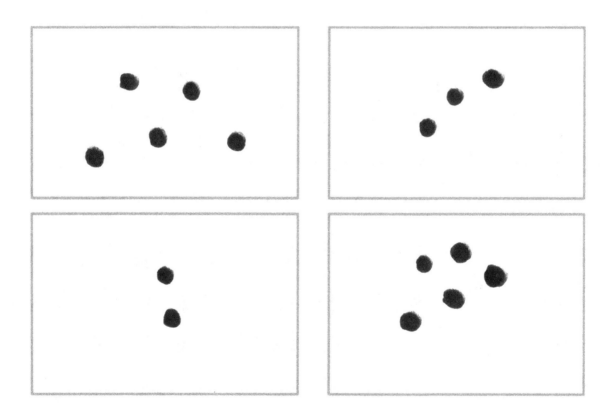

PIZZA

On the following pages are pizza pies. There are slices with pepperoni on them. And the ones without pepperoni on them are the slices that have been eaten or missing.

PIZZA

How many slices are in each pie? How many slices are missing?

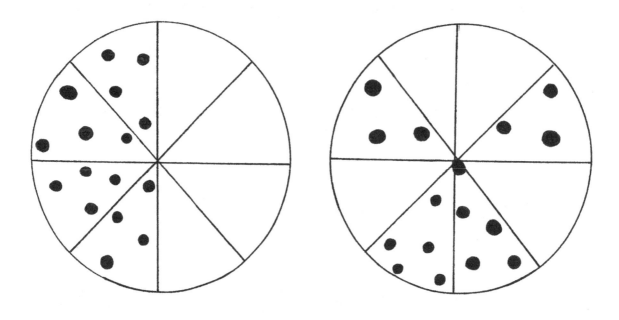

Slices_____   Missing _____

PIZZA

How many slices are in each pie? How many slices are missing?

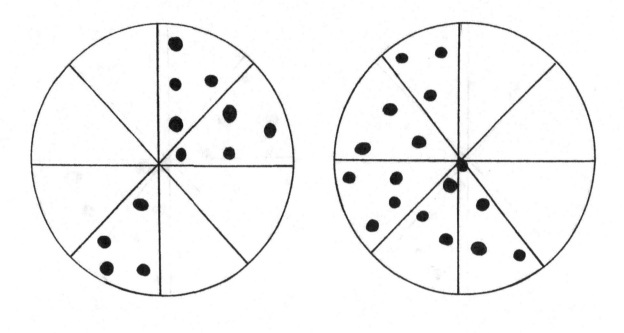

Slices_____   Missing _____

PIZZA

How many slices are in each pie? How many slices are missing?

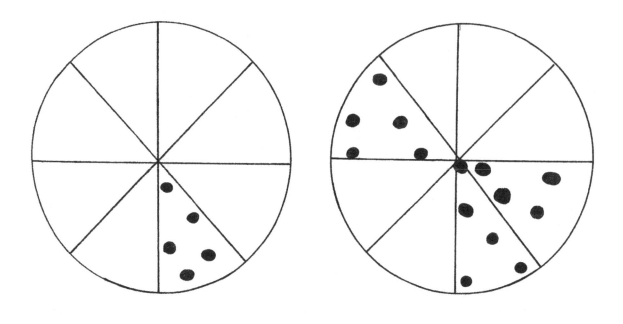

Slices_____   Missing _____

TELLING TIME

Sandy Mouse is learning how to read a clock. Help her match the times to the clock by circling the clock that shows the time written on the left.

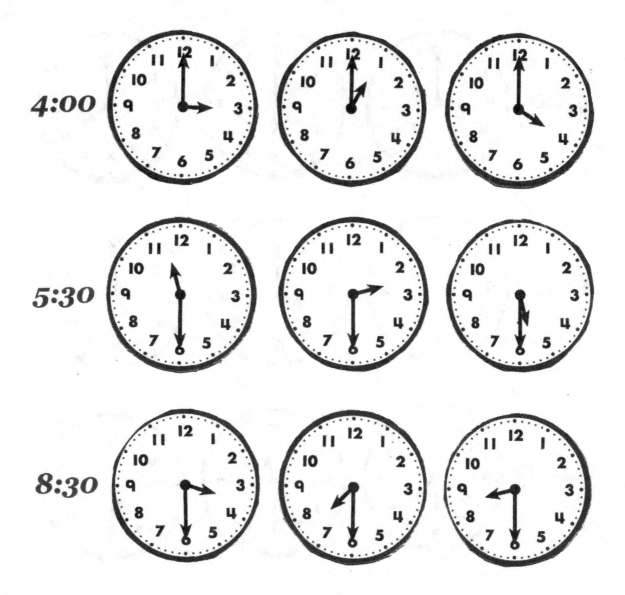

4:00

5:30

8:30

TELLING TIME

Sandy Mouse is learning how to read a clock. Help her match the times to the clock by circling the clock that shows the time written on the left.

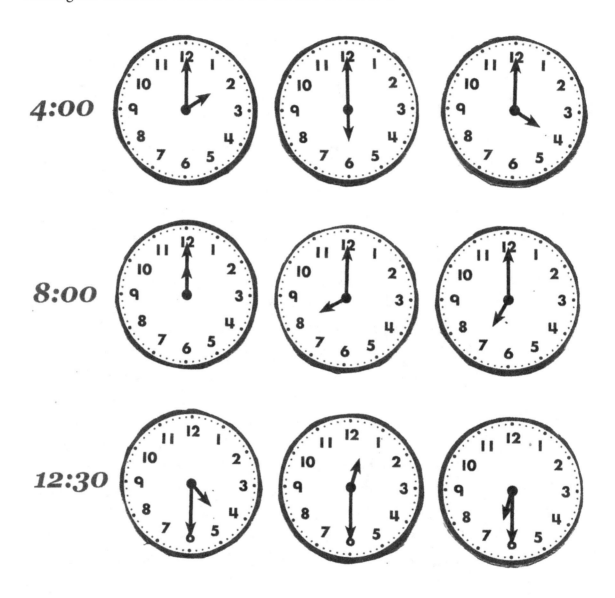

4:00

8:00

12:30

TELLING TIME

Sandy Mouse is learning how to read a clock. Help her match the times to the clock by circling the clock that shows the time written on the left.

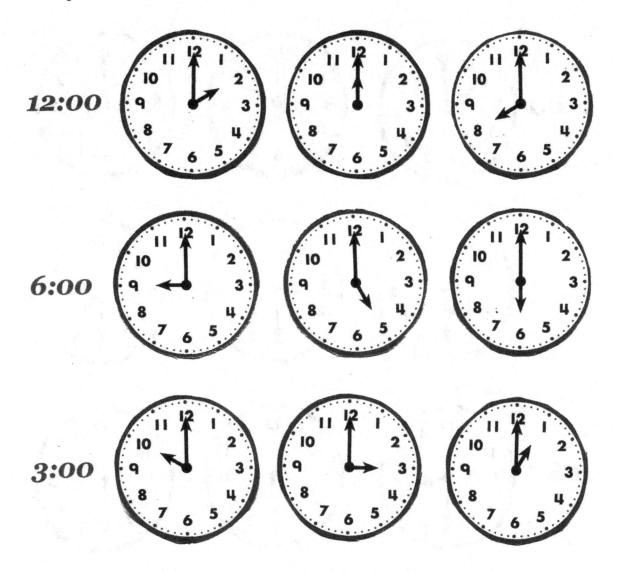

12:00

6:00

3:00

TELLING TIME

Sandy Mouse is learning how to read a clock. Help her match the times to the clock by circling the clock that shows the time written on the left.

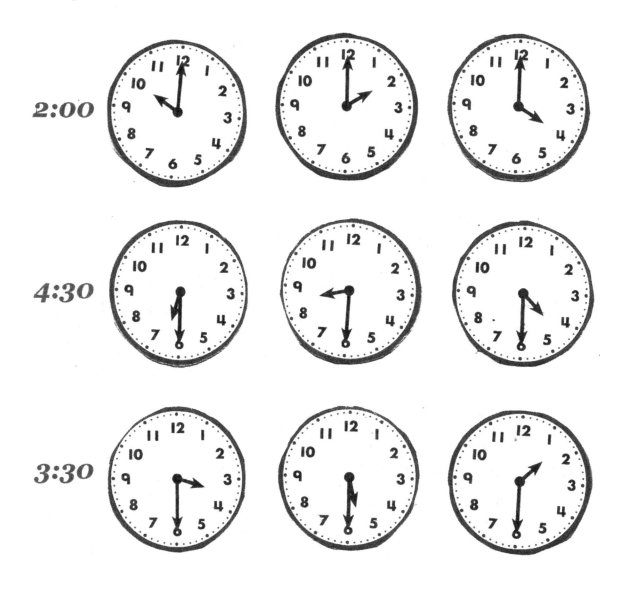

2:00

4:30

3:30

TELLING TIME

Sandy Mouse is learning how to read a clock. Help her match the times to the clock by circling the clock that shows the time written on the left.

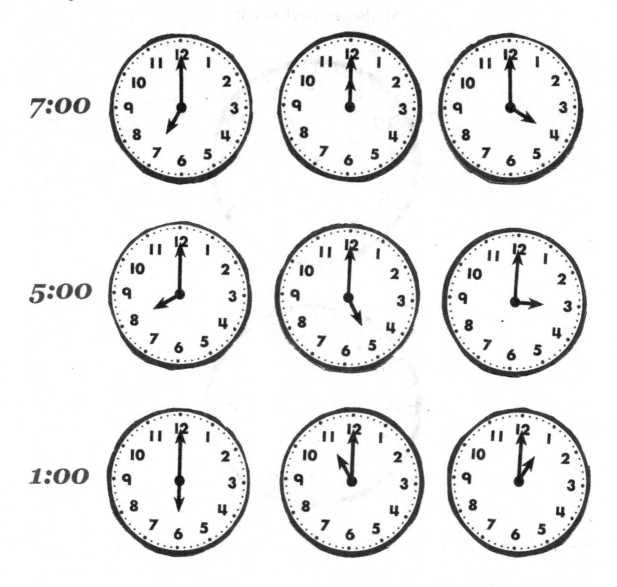

7:00

5:00

1:00

TIME

Set the clocks below.
Set the first clock to 7:30.
Set the next clock to 1:30.

TIME

Set the clocks below.
Set the first clock to 2:00.
Set the next clock to 5:30.

TIME

Set the clocks below.
Set the first clock to 9:00.
Set the next clock to 10:30.

TIME

Set the clocks below.
Set the first clock to 3:00.
Set the next clock to 1:30.

TIME

Set the clocks below.
Set the first clock to 6:00.
Set the next clock to 8:30.

A.M. OR P.M.

a.m. means "before midday" (12 o'clock at night to 12 o'clock noon). p.m. means "after midday" (12 o'clock noon to 12 o'clock at night). Read the sentences and write whether the events happened in the a.m. or p.m. The first statement is an example.

STATEMENT	ANSWER
Mikey and Justin leave for school at 7 o'clock every morning.	_a.m._
Our plane will take off before noon.	_____
Chelsea loves our bed time stories.	_____
Billy and his cousins will start a campfire.	_____
They all come back from school in the afternoon.	_____
At 8 o'clock, grandma cooks eggs for everybody's breakfast.	_____
Every day we get together and watch television after dinner.	_____
On Saturday mornings, everyone cuts grass.	_____

101

PRACTICE RECOGNIZING PATTERNS

How many sixes are there?
How many eights are there?
How many ones are there?

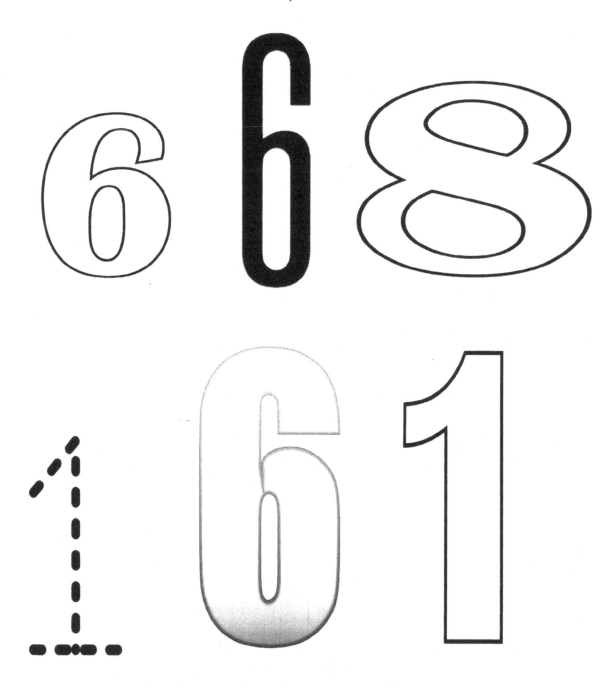

PRACTICE RECOGNIZING PATTERNS

How many sevens are there?
How many fours are there?
How many twos are there?
How many zeros are there?

PRACTICE RECOGNIZING PATTERNS

How many nines are there?
How many threes are there?
How many fives are there?
How many twos are there?

5 3 5 2

9 2 9 5

PRACTICE RECOGNIZING PATTERNS

How many rockets are there?
How many stars are there?

PRACTICE RECOGNIZING PATTERNS

How many happy-face stars are there?
How many plain stars are there?

PRACTICE RECOGNIZING PATTERNS

How many umbrellas are there?
How many dog bones are there?

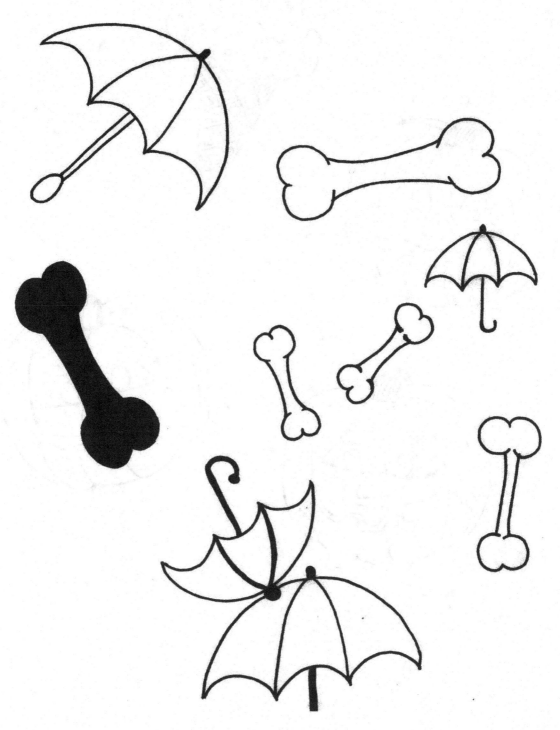

WHICH PICTURE IS DIFFERENT?

WHICH PICTURE IS DIFFERENT?

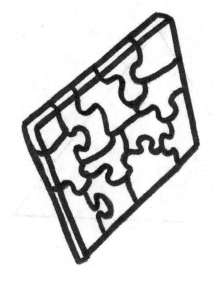

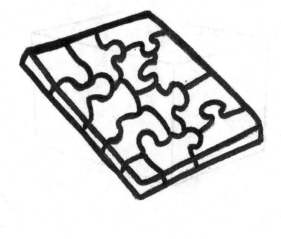

WHICH PICTURE IS DIFFERENT?

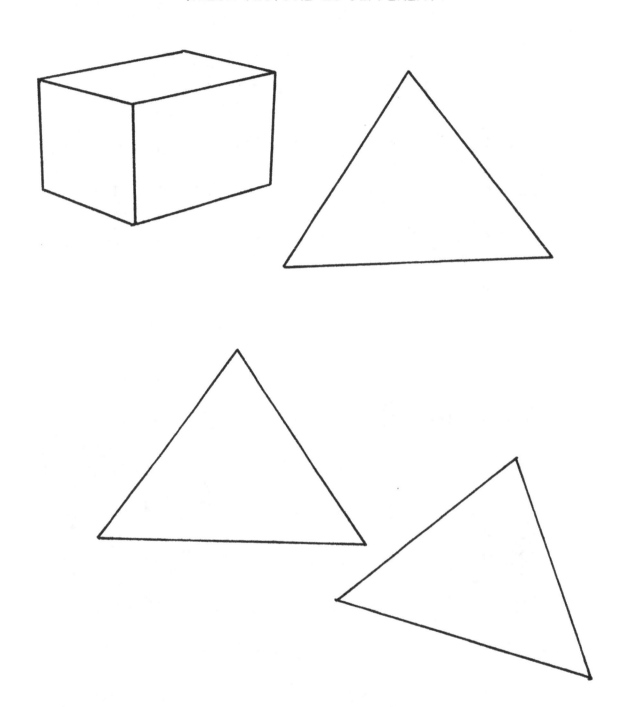

WHICH PICTURE IS DIFFERENT?

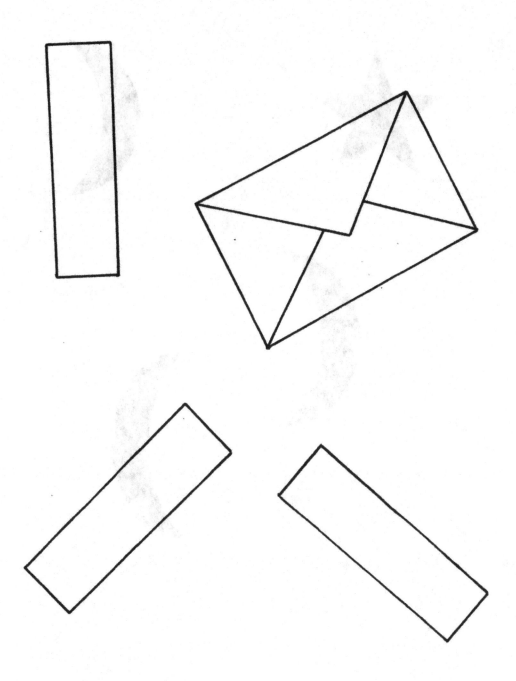

WHICH PICTURE IS DIFFERENT?

THE BALD EAGLE AND THE UNITED STATES OF AMERICA FLAG

The Bald Eagle is the National Emblem of the United States of America. The Bald Eagle was chosen as the National Symbol of the United States in 1782. The American Flag symbolizes our country's strength and unity. It consists of 13 horizontal stripes, and seven red and six white. The stripes represent the original 13 colonies. The stars are white with a blue background, and they represent the 50 states of the union.

THE LIBERTY BELL

The word *Pennsylvania* is misspelled on the bell. On the bell it is spelled "Pensylvania".

NEIL ARMSTRONG

Born August 5, 1930, Command Pilot for Gemini 8, Mission Commander on Apollo 11, and the first person to stand on the moon.

PRESIDENT GEORGE WASHINGTON

George Washington was the first President of the United States of America.

KENNEDY SPACE CENTER

The first manned NASA shuttle was launched from Kennedy Space Center in 1968. The crew of the Apollo 8 were the first human beings to exit Earth's orbit, travel around the moon and back.

WASHINGTON MONUMENT

This monument was completed in 1884, and it is a tribute to the first U.S. President, George Washington. It is 555 feet tall.

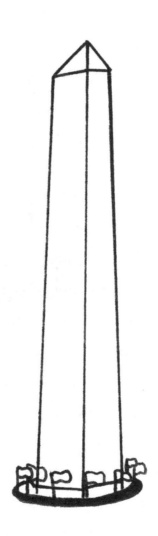

CAN YOU NAME ANY STATES?

Which state do you live in?

SPORTS

Can you identify the sports on the following pages?
Which sports do you like to play?

SPORTS

Name this sport.

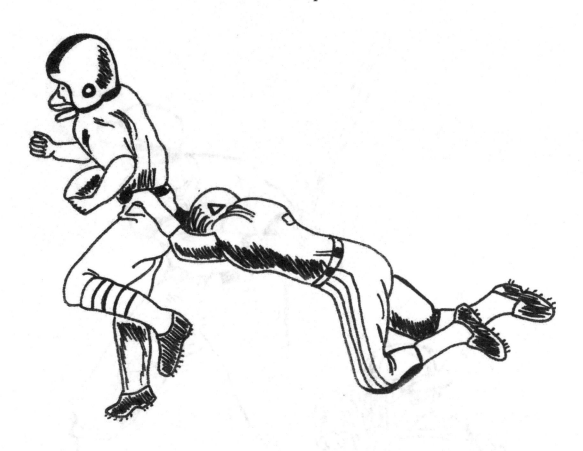

SPORTS

Name this sport.

SPORTS

Name this sport.

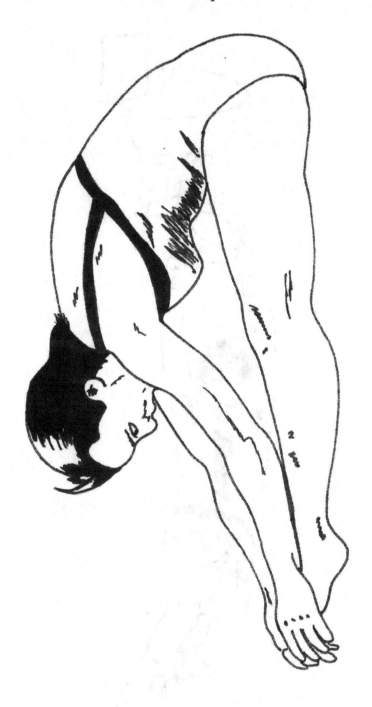

SPORTS

Name this sport.

SPORTS

Name this sport.

FIND THE ANIMAL BELOW THAT IS DIFFERENT FROM THE OTHERS.

FIND THE ANIMAL BELOW THAT IS DIFFERENT FROM THE OTHERS.

FIND THE ANIMAL BELOW THAT IS DIFFERENT FROM THE OTHERS.

CAN YOU NAME THE ITEMS BELOW THAT LIVE IN THE OCEAN?

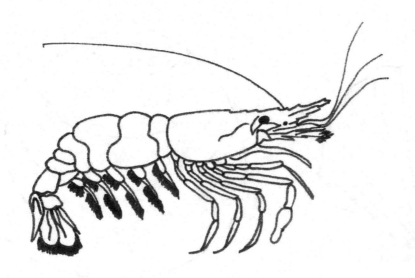

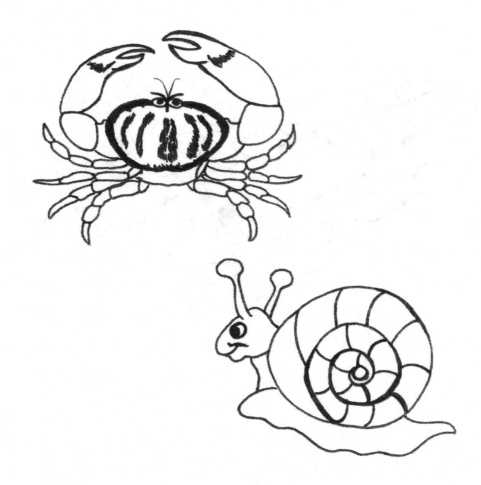

CAN YOU NAME THE ITEMS BELOW THAT LIVE IN THE OCEAN?

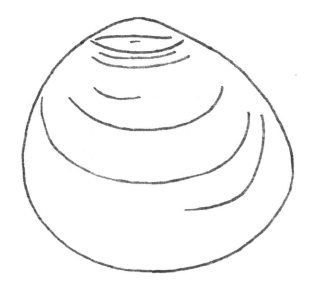
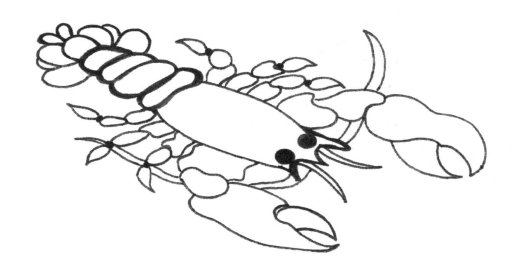

HAVE YOU SEEN ANY OF THE ANIMALS BELOW IN YOUR YARD?

Say the names to the ones you have.

IDENTIFY THE ANIMALS BELOW

IDENTIFY THE ANIMALS BELOW

IDENTIFY THE ANIMALS BELOW

IDENTIFY THE ANIMALS BELOW

IDENTIFY THE ANIMALS BELOW

IDENTIFY THE ANIMALS BELOW

IDENTIFY THE ANIMALS BELOW

IDENTIFY THE ANIMALS BELOW

IDENTIFY THE ANIMALS BELOW

HOLIDAYS

Do you know what holiday each picture stands for on the following pages? Which holiday or holidays are your favorite?

NAMING VEHICLES

Can you name the vehicles people use to travel below and on the following page?

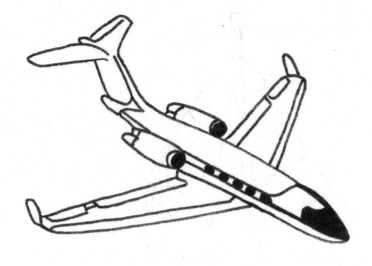

NAMING VEHICLES

Can you name the vehicles people use to travel below and on the following page?

WHICH ONE FLIES INTO ORBIT?

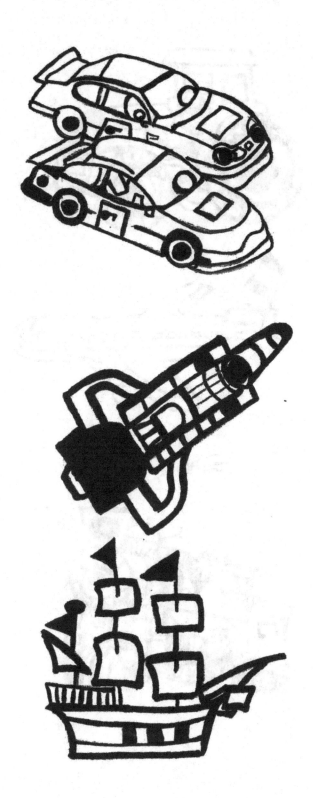

WHICH ONE BLOWS A WHISTLE?

CAN YOU IDENTIFY THE PEOPLE BELOW?

Which one is the policewoman?
Which one is the mail carrier?
And which one is the fireman?

WHAT ARE THE LITTLE BOYS SITTING ON?

FUN THINGS

1. What do you use when it's raining?
   umbrella   or   frying pan

2. What do you put on your head when it's cold outside?
   hat   or   shoes

3. What do you put on your feet when it's snowing outside?
   boots   or   boxes

4. What can you wear when it's warm outside?
   shorts   or   pants

5. What do you take off when you go into the pool?
   socks and shoes   or   a book

6. What do you brush before you go to bed?
   hair   or   your teeth

7. What do you put on your hands when it's cold outside?
   gloves   or   slippers

8. What do Daddy and Mommy wash the floor with?
   box   or   mop

9. What do horses eat?
   hay   or   cookies

10. Where do you pump air into on a bicycle?
    seat   or   tires

11. What animal has black stripes?

   zebra   or   pig

12. What can you give Mommy for a present?

   flowers   or   beach ball

13. What do you put on when it's cold outside to keep warm?

   pajamas   or   a coat

14. What do Daddy and Mommy drive when they take you places?

   cars and trucks   or   a scooter

15. What do children wait for in the mornings to go to school?

   school bus   or   horse

16. What do children pull behind them?

   wagon   or   ball

17. What do Daddy and Mommy sweep the floor with?

   broom   or   stick

18. What animals do kids want to bring home for pets?

   cats and dogs   or   an elephant

19. What do kids like to watch on television?

   cartoons   or   movies

20. What do you use when you color in your coloring books?

   pens   or   crayons

21. Who climbs down the chimney at Christmas?

   Easter Bunny   or   Santa Claus

22. What do most people eat on Thanksgiving?

    turkey   or   bacon

23. What color is always used on Valentine's Day?

    blue   or   red

24. What do you color for Easter?

    eggs   or   cereal

25. Where do most people go on Easter morning?

    shopping   or   church

26. When you are in class, who mostly writes on the chalkboard?

    teacher   or   principal

27. What smells pretty?

    flowers   or   bugs

28. What would be more fun taking a trip in?

    choo-choo train   or   bus

29. What would you help Daddy and Mommy do?

    take out the garbage   or   pick up my toys

MORE QUESTIONS

1. What can you plant in the garden?
   vegetables   socks   fruits   shoes

2. What shoots from the sky?
   kitten   dog   star   shoes

3. What can leap farther?
   bird   duck   worm   frog

4. What food is sweet?
   onions   candy   meatloaf   eggs

5. What gets tired when you walk them too much?
   dogs   fish   shoes   cars

6. What sport do you use a softball for?
   golf   basketball   tennis   softball

7. What must you wear at the beach?
   bananas   sunscreen   coat   curlers

8. Where can you build a sandcastle?
   bathtub   beach   pool   car

9. What do animals love to drink when they are very thirsty?
   Coca-Cola   orange juice   water   milk

10. Where are lifeguards usually working?
    grocery store   bank   swimming pool   kitchen

11. What game do you play when there's a net at the beach?
    hockey   golf   volleyball

12. What do people usually do when someone is taking their picture?
    smile   turn your head   yell

13. What is really big and cute and lives in the ocean?
    fish   dolphin

14. What do children love to learn how to ride?
    rocking chair   swing   bicycle

15. Which animal has big ears?
    giraffe   monkey   elephant

16. What bear is black and white?
    teddy bear   panda bear

17. What always lives in the woods and has antlers?
    deer   monkey   snake

18. What bird lives in a tree and hoots?
    jaybird   cardinal   owl

19. What is the animal that has stripes?
    pony   donkey   zebra

20. What do you take a ride in when you are in the ocean?
    car   plane   boat

21. When someone hands you something what do you say?
    "hello"   "thank you"   "let's eat"

22. What do people wear on their heads?

   hats   cowboy boots   pennies

23. Do umbrellas have holes in them?

   yes   no

24. How many legs does a flamingo usually stand on?

   one   two

25. What does a turtle usually hide under when it is scared?

   rock   tree   shell

THE FOUR SEASONS

On the following pages are a list of activities for you to do when school is out. Add some of the ideas that you like to do to the list.

SPRING

Things to do when school is out.

Plant Some Flowers
Read a Book
Have a Game Night
Do Some Baking
Start a Vegetable Garden
Fly a Kite
Make a Photo Album
Go Fishing
Play Hopscotch
Do Some Painting
Go Horseback Riding
Make a Bird Feeder
Go Hiking

SUMMER

Things to do when school is out

Watch the Fireworks
Go to the Beach
Go Swimming
Play Some Sports
Read A Book
Go Bike Riding
Camp Out in Your Back Yard
Play Games with Your Friends
Go To The Zoo
Go On A Trip
Build a Bonfire At The Beach
Help Work In Your Yard

FALL

Things to do when school is out.

Make Apple Cider
Walk a Corn Maze
Do some Holiday Baking
Watch Movies
Play in the Snow
Go Sledding
Read a Book
Pick Some Apples
Go to a Football Game
Donate Some Things to a Shelter
Make a Costume for Halloween
Give Away Some Candy
Go Christmas Shopping

WINTER

Things to do when school is out.

Make an Ornament
Have an Icicle Fight
Give a Secret Gift to Someone
Make a Snowman
Go Ice Skating
Make a Gingerbread House
Build Your Own Sled
Make a Snow Angel
Listen to Carolers
Make Hot Chocolate
Sit by the Fire and Read a Book
Help Decorate the Christmas Tree
Hang Some Christmas Lights

CHELSEA AND THE DOLPHIN

Once upon a time, there was a girl named Chelsea. She lived close to the sea. Her parents often took her to the beach, but they warned her never to go by herself.

She and Mikey would play in the sea. Chelsea wanted to swim in the deep, but her parents never let her.

Drifting, she yelled, "Help! Help!"

No one heard her cries, and she went under.

Suddenly, a dolphin came and pushed her to the surface. She gasped the sweet air. Pushing and prodding, the dolphin guided her to the shallows. Then the dolphin turned and was gone.

Her parents noticed Chelsea was missing. They looked and looked in the house, but they did not see Chelsea. Running outside, they yelled her name and spotted her coming out of the sea. They ran toward the beach and yelled, "Chelsea, Chelsea." But Chelsea kept staring at the water and waving at the jumping dolphin.

"Mommy and Daddy, the dolphin saved me!"

Mikey said, "Sure it did."

Chelsea said, "I promise you. The dolphin saved me."

"Chelsea, don't ever come out here alone," Daddy scolded.

"Yes, Daddy," Chelsea said.

The dolphin watched from the sea as the strange creatures walked away.

DOUGHNUT

Stacey and Mia wanted to go to the doughnut shop. Stacy and Mia went to Stacy's house to break open her piggy bank so they could buy some doughnuts. The doughnut shop was just around the corner from Stacy's house. The girls were so excited about finally getting some doughnuts. They walked, skipped, and daydream about the sweet treats.

When Stacey and Mia finally reached the doughnut shop, they saw a hungry puppy around the side of the shop. It was looking for food. When the girls saw how hungry the puppy was, they agreed to buy the puppy a doughnut too. Mia stayed outside with the puppy while Stacy went inside to buy the doughnuts. When Stacy came out of the doughnut shop with the doughnuts, the little puppy was hopping up and down in happiness.

The girls ate their doughnuts, watched the puppy eat his doughnut, and began loving this little puppy. Stacy wanted to take the puppy home.

When she brought the puppy into the house, her mom took one look at the puppy and said, "Oh no, Stacy. That looks like a mean dog."

"Please, Mom, I'll take great care of him."

"I don't know, Stacy. You will have to ask your father when he comes home."

Later that day, Stacy's father came home. He loved the puppy as soon as he saw him. He loved the puppy so much that he named him Doughnut because of the circle around his eye. Little Doughnut hit the lottery that day and lived a long and happy life with his new family.

I hope you have gotten some helpful insights into the needs of autistic and other special-needs children. The cause and/or causes of autism are still unknown. If science can discover what causes this dreadful disease, then perhaps it can be eliminated. I pray so.

Dawn Adams

Printed in the United States
By Bookmasters